WITNESS PREPARATION
A Manual for Attorneys

Allan Campo

with Stuart Simon and Todd Betanzos

ISBN-13: 978-1463741662

ISBN-10: 1463741669

Contents:

Exercises:

Introduction

This short manual will help you to prepare your witnesses for making testimony at deposition and at trial. We have tried to make it practical. No fat. Since ninety percent of testimony preparation is for deposition, you will find it over-balanced in that direction. Our practice is entirely civil litigation, thus, the book is oriented towards civil cases. Further, it focuses more upon the preparation of fact witnesses than experts, although expert witnesses will certainly need the skills taught here. Finally, it presupposes that the witnesses being prepared by you are important to the case, key players who will be tasked with explaining essential matters.

Put simply, this manual is intended to give you some tools to help you do what most civil attorneys spend most of the time actually doing with important fact witnesses: finding out what they know, helping them think about how to testify to it clearly and accurately, and preparing them for questioning at deposition by an adverse party's attorney. While it is not essential to do so, this book can be paired with the author's more general handbook on precision communication, *Hotseat*. We suggest that you consider giving your prospective witness a copy of that handbook. Certainly, that might make the handbook discoverable. However, take a look at it before you get uncomfortable. Few attorneys would quibble with the values espoused in the handbook.

This manual is written in bullet point style as a series of tips and suggestions. For efficiency, we have used "he", "him" and "his" to refer to persons of either gender throughout. There are many short exercises that are designed to help you teach important concepts to your witnesses. We hope the style of this book makes it user-friendly, easier to pick up and put back down, and that it becomes a reference to which you return again and again.

The Core Concept:
Developing Testifying Skills

• Testifying to the truth relies mostly upon learned communication skills. We tell testifiers that they are not there to rely upon their native ability to "tell it like it is", because, ironically, "telling it like it is", the way most people do it, anyway, often makes for poor testimony. Witnesses are not at a deposition or at trial to "tell" something; they are there to answer questions. Telling and answering are different. Explain this to your witness early and remind him/her of it frequently.

Here's what is said about testimony in the handbook, *Hotseat*:

"Speaking with the discipline required of legal testimony is a unique form of communication. It occurs under conditions unlike any other. Too many people have gone into important communications settings armed with the best of intentions and a determination to "just speak the truth", or to "just tell it like it is", only to have great difficulty doing it successfully. Their words are misunderstood. They make misstatements. They get confused. They haven't thought systematically about the experiences they'll be asked to address. They are not fully prepared for the careful questioning they encounter."

• You will want to establish with your witness very early that mere knowledge of the facts and a commitment to truthfulness is far from sufficient to prepare for giving testimony. Wait, isn't truthfulness the most important thing? Absolutely! Commitment to the truth is the foundation of this training method. Testimony is truthful communication assembled like a model of a ship, all the pieces joined correctly, and the vessel presented in perfect scale to the actual.

• It's all about getting your witness to talk through the facts carefully and in detail, and answering your questions. Then, doing it again and again. (And a few more times…) Communications experts teach us that repeated telling of a story creates increased efficiency. Speakers start to find better descriptive words, smoother elements of transition, shorter and clearer explanations.

• You should work with your witness on finding the right language to communicate key elements of the truth. Of course, you should never tell him what to say, and we trust that you will not. But, neither should you abandon him at this critical time. Help him find strong words and encourage him to use them. Witnesses are not trained speakers or writers. Many do not even own a dictionary or a thesaurus. Yet, surely, your witness deserves to have the full power of the English language available to him for making his testimony! He is there to speak the truth — and he ought to have the words to do it clearly.

• Have a dictionary in the room when you prep with your witness; have a thesaurus available. If his language selection is not clear, ask him to look up meanings of words, search for synonyms, etc. You will love the "Aha!" look on the face of your witness when he finds the right way to describe something; the words that perfectly capture his sense of the truth of it.

• Do not think of this manual as a tool for putting a favorable "spin" on the truth. If anything, the approach suggested here is anti-spin, because "spinning a story" usually means telling a version of the story that most favors you, no matter how well or poorly it tracks with the truth. "Spinning" is selecting words for effect rather than for accuracy. The power of the approach taught here lies in the credibility a witness earns through clear and honest telling of his experience. The potent effect of candor and sincerity itself is all that you or he should seek.

• Hearing questions on a topic more than once (many times more than once!) helps a testifier tune his ear to the key elements and/or flag words in the questions, thus helping him recognize traps in those questions and how to answer them. You are teaching your witness as much to listen with precision as to speak with it. Make sure you give him lots of time to learn to listen to and respond to both the style and the substance of questions he will face.

• You are probably getting the point that the Core Concept is repetition. There should be repeated conversations about the facts and how most clearly to speak to them. There should be repeated opportunities for the witness to answer questions asked in an adverse style. That is the key to success.

• Your contacts with any particular witness about his testimony should not follow one immediately upon another. Witness preparation meetings should be scheduled at intervals so that witnesses can digest and think about what they have covered. Further, they will need to organize their recollections and store them efficiently in long-term memory. You can facilitate this process by doing your witness preparation in several half-day meetings with at least one or more days in-between.

• A popular variation on this interval-learning protocol for witnesses is to prepare two witnesses simultaneously (though usually not in one another's presence), one in the morning and one in the afternoon, on several days. This method also reduces the negative impact of fatigue.

• Witness preparation may necessarily involve some last minute "cramming" into short-term memory on the eve of deposition or trial testimony. But this type of preparation should be limited to refreshing your witness' recall of the details of documents or email strings and that sort of thing- not to the key facts and arguments in the case. Keep this important distinction in mind.

The Central Theme: The Truth. The Whole Truth. Nothing but the Truth.

• The preparation of any particular witness should emerge from that witness' authentic sense for what is true. In the communications handbook, *Hotseat*, there is a section that explains this:

"Your knowledge — your truth — is based on what you saw and heard and felt and thought. Your testimony is the words you use to speak to your truth, to explain it. Others may have seen and heard and felt and thought something different, even at the same place and time. Their sense of the truth will be different, and, if so, their words probably will be different, too."

The handbook also says this:

"A useful idea to understand is that there is frequently a difference between the objective truth (an empirically verifiable phenomenon) and subjective truth (what a particular person experiences and believes). Sometimes the two truths seem much different. While you may have some confidence that you know what is objectively true, you can only speak with certainty to your own subjective truth."

• You need not be disappointed nor should your witness feel badly if his sense for what is true does not precisely match that of other witnesses. This is the way the world actually works! Help your witness speak thoughtfully and without embarrassment to the distinctions between his view and that of others. This will only increase his credibility.

• Learn the construct below and teach it to your witnesses:

The Elements of Testimony

The Truth: The facts to which the witness can testify, with appropriate characterizations.

The Whole Truth: Context and background information that gives the facts meaning.

Nothing but the Truth: What the witness knows to be NOT true.

• Learn the construct below and teach it to your witnesses:

The Testifier's Task

Report and Characterize the Facts: (*The Truth*)

Give The Facts Context, Background, and Meaning: (*The Whole Truth*)

Defend the Facts from Inaccuracy and Mischaracterization: (*Nothing But the Truth*)

• The rest of this manual is designed to help you teach your witnesses how to accomplish the testifier's task.

First Things First:
Appearance and Behavior

• You should help your witness be more relaxed by answering his questions and responding to his concerns. Please make sure to signal respect for the worries of a witness. If he is feeling it, it is real. You need to help him with it. Let's look at what is said in the handbook, *Hotseat*:

"Witnesses in legal testimony usually have special meetings with their attorneys to prepare for testimony. If you are going to be a witness in a lawsuit, it is best that you discuss the specifics of the case only with your lawyer. Otherwise, these principles apply to all key communication assignments where precision and accuracy are essential.

Get someone to help you prepare for your communication "moment". Speak about any concerns you may have, however great or small. Be systematic. Get him/her to make a list of issues and then address them together, one at a time. Even worries that seem silly or irrational can drain your energy and make it more difficult for you to feel confident when it is time to step up, so make sure to talk about them all!"

• Assist your witness in addressing any and all sources of anxiety and distraction, as they will take energy away from him and reduce his ability to testify. He needs to be feeling as good as he can feel when he takes on this task. It can be daunting.

• Witnesses ought to look good when making testimony. This old saw is supported by hard science. People who are judged to be attractive: neat, appropriately dressed, body erect, head up, with smiles on their faces - are also judged to be more credible.

• Witnesses who look good feel good. More science: When a person's self-image is more favorable, when they believe they look "good" to others, they feel happier and more confident.

• Many depositions (and more trials) are recorded on video. You should think about your witness as a guest on a television program. How can she look her best for that event? Generally, if you prepare for all depositions as though they will be video recorded, you will be doing the better thing.

• Help your witnesses make good decisions about how to dress for their testimony. Have them get their hair cut and/or styled. Be very direct about this topic. Have an on-purpose conversation with them about what they will wear for their testimony. If you are not absolutely sure that you know how a particular witness will be dressed get him, at some point before the testimony, to use his phone or camera to take a picture of the clothing he proposes to wear so that you can see it. Your witnesses can only benefit from these efforts.

• Attorneys questioning well-dressed and neat-appearing witnesses are generally more deferential and less aggressive. This is not a unique statement about attorneys. Rather, it is a consequence of human nature.

• Sometimes you will hear attorneys say, "A witness who is a plumber should look like a plumber". Generally, we disagree. What you really want for your witnesses is for them to feel at their best. Occasionally, that will mean witnesses elect to wear their occupation's signature clothing - a policeman in his uniform, for example – but proceed carefully in this matter. Witnesses are usually more confident and resourceful when they are well-dressed. They are also less likely to be stereotyped by either the questioner or the audience.

• Acclimate your witness to the setting for his testimony. Deposition testimony, for example is usually made with a witness sitting at the end of a conference table. Attorneys position themselves on either side, with the questioning attorney(s) facing the defending attorney(s). If there is a camera for recording, it will usually be at the far end of the table. The witness and the attorneys will usually be wearing small clip-on microphones. The entire scene will seem very strange to most witnesses. If you control where the deposition will occur, prepare your witness in the same room and in the same seat he will sit in for the actual event, so that he will become comfortable with the surroundings.

• If possible, provide a heavy solid chair with a tall back and good armrests so that the witness will have the most secure seat in the room. Not too soft. The chair that is best is almost throne-like in it's re-assuring effect upon someone sitting in it. Avoid those rocking, swiveling, wheeled conference-room chairs! They are the opposite of what a witness needs. Strength. Stability. Security. That's what you are after.

• Seat your witness in the chair and move it close to the table. Show him how to lean slightly forward over the table, placing his forearms and hands on the table in the manner of a newscaster or television announcer. This is the most attractive posture. Witnesses seated in this fashion are "leaning into the action'; they are engaged, involved. With hands showing, they are sending a message of open-ness and willingness to disclose. This is not a manipulation. Your witness should be feeling open and willing to disclose! If you and he prepare thoroughly, this will be exactly the case.

• A testifying witness should learn to keep his head upright and his forearms and hands on the table. This keeps the upper body more quiet and stable. He should not wave his hands about. He shouldn't touch his face or hair, adjust his clothing, or pick at imaginary strands of lint. Certainly, he should not hide his hands under the table. If he practices managing his upper body in this way and becomes accustomed to it, he will remain more comfortable over the long haul, and will be better-rested and less likely to tense up when the questioning gets tough, and it usually does.

• When handed a document, the witness should keep one forearm down while using the other hand to manage the document. This helps to maintain an upright and stable posture.

• We have said for many years that the witness should strive to be the nicest person in the room. You should explain to your witnesses that their actions and demeanor are as much evidence of credibility as any words they speak. Relax and smile. Smile and relax.

• If a deposition becomes an argument between attorneys, as sometimes happens, the witness should remain quiet and out of the fray. Further, witnesses should avoid being drawn into even the most innocuous of side conversations during a deposition. Finally, witnesses shouldn't try to make jokes - ever. We say to witnesses that they should find the most serenely agreeable version of themselves and bring that to the deposition.

• You should explain that a good witness is like a peach: soft and sweet on the outside; solid as a rock on the inside. That's what confidence in the truth, and the ability to speak to it, will bring to your witness.

The Truth-
Keep It Short & Simple (K.I.S.S.)

Word Selection: Naming and Characterizing Things

• The first principle we teach with regard to testimony is that speaking the truth requires precise language. Poets and writers of prose will search long and hard for the one word that captures the essence- the truth- about a flower or a sunrise or a person. You and your witness may need to do the same with her testimony.

• It is easier to think about a thing when you have a word for it. It is easier to communicate about it, too. Sometimes we relate this story:

"I used to tell my kids that nobody ever bought cheeseburgers until somebody gave them a simple name. Why? In a very serious tone I would explain to them that it was very risky to walk into a restaurant and say that you wanted ""one-of-those-hot-ground-beef-patties-grilled-and-then-placed-on-a-round-bun-with-a-slice-of-cheddar-cheese-on-top-and-some-lettuce-and-tomato-and-ketchup-too! It was very easy for the person ordering to get part of that thirty-word formula wrong and end up with who knows what on a sandwich! It was also too easy for the person taking the order to miss one or two words of the order and prepare it incorrectly! Plus, everybody got really tired, just trying to order lunch…

Clearly, there was a need for a single unique word that immediately communicated everything the hungry customer wanted. It would need to be a word that the customer could give to an order-taker who then knew exactly what was being requested. Finally, along came a brilliant child who said, "Let's call it a 'cheeseburger'"! Ah… The world became a better place!

The kids loved the story and instantly saw the lesson. After all, kids are always asking, "What is that, Mom?", "What do you call that thing over there, Dad?" I bet your witness will get it, too."

• It is typical in lawsuits to find one or more elements of the case that need to be called *something*. Sometimes an event is easier to talk about if it is named, given a title, or assigned what we sometimes call a "tag". A language expert might say that an important event begs for a "nominal". That moment when two key individuals first come into one another's presence? Is it the "Introduction", the "Encounter", the "Discovery", the "Meeting", the "Confrontation"? What title most clearly captures the important qualities of the event? Figuring out and introducing useful names for case elements is a very worthwhile exercise for both attorneys and witnesses. These names help witnesses speak to the elements concisely and accurately; but, more importantly, names help listeners.

• The terms for nominals are often used interchangeably. We, though, have developed the habit of thinking of nominals as a heirarchy: "Titles" are for key events or circumstances ("The Baby's Illness"). "Names" are for lesser events, unique situational dynamics ("Local Rivalry"). "Tags" are usually reserved for objects (that old favorite: "The Accident Vehicle").

• Listeners use titles of events like the titles of chapters in a book; they are tools for organizing the story. The best ones are easy to remember, to carry around. We call this "portability". Good titles also pack rich imagery and help listeners recall the associated facts and arguments. We call this "capacity". A good title has both portability and capacity.

The "Titles" Exercise

Take five minutes and do this no-stress teaching drill with your witness. It will be enjoyable and will help to drive home the Importance and the utility of titles for situations and events.

Ask your witness what comes to mind when these famous event titles are used:

"The Cold War"

"9/11"

"D-Day"

Notice together the richness of the imagery, how many things you and he can recall simply by bringing up the familiar title of something!

Now, ask your witness what comes to mind when he thinks of one of these common life-event names:

"My Graduation"

"My Wedding"

"My Best Vacation"

Notice again, how much detail and richness of imagery can come up for you simply by invoking the title of an event!

• Many lawsuits (and almost all criminal cases) have one or more situations and/or events that would benefit from being named so that attorneys, witnesses, and fact-finders can organize and remember the associated information.

• Brainstorm with your witness. What are the key moments in the story of your case? What are the key situations? What are the issues? What are the disagreements? Do these things need to be titled or named?

• You add great power to your case if you (in argument) or your witness (in testimony) are the first to assign nominals to things. You will be able to make sure that these titles and names capture the essence of the thing. You will be able to make sure that they are portable and capacious. We say to attorneys and witnesses: "If you name it- you can tame it." We also say, "If you name it- you can claim it."

• Keep this idea in mind: If neither you nor your witness assign accurate and useful nominals to key events, situations, and objects (and arguments - arguments can be named, too!) somebody will. It might be opposing counsel, it might be a witness for the other side, it could be a juror. That name which you didn't pick might mischaracterize the truth, unfairly color an event, or distort reality, and it might be a key to persuading a fact-finder.

• Sometimes one-word titles aren't sufficient to capture the real essence of the thing being named. For example, "accident" may not be enough. It may take "chain-reaction accident" or "high-speed accident" to deliver the full picture. If the essence of the event is not its dynamic so much as its effect, it might more truthfully be expressed as the "horrific accident" or (much different) that "unfortunate accident". Do not be tempted, through the use of such potent modifiers, to try to render a swan from an inescapably ugly duckling. Evocative adjectives and adverbs rarely work very well for listeners unless they help to drive home the truth. If they are used disingenuously, they typically ring sour, like a bad bell. Everybody hears it - and everybody grimaces.

• Descriptive words in testimony are more effective when they are few in number and have been thoughtfully selected for their capacity to illuminate a point sincerely addressed. When thus used, they sparkle, and draw the listener's ear to the speaker's words. There is for the listener a reward: a flash of color, a surge of feeling.

The "Thesaurus" Exercise

Take five minutes and do this no-stress teaching drill with your witness. It will help to drive home for him the importance of word selection when seeking precision and accuracy in descriptive language. We usually call these terms "characterizations".

Ask him how many words or phrases he can think of that have more or less the same meaning as the word "nice" (with regard to a person). Offer him a dictionary or thesaurus as an aid. Then make a list together.

Here's some examples we found:

Nice: pleasant, likable, agreeable, personable, congenial, amiable, affable, genial, friendly, charming, delightful, engaging; sympathetic, simpatico, compassionate, good, polite, courteous, civil, refined, polished, genteel, elegant.

Now, ask him to think about a "nice" person he knows and request that he select the word from the list that captures the essence of that person's "nice-ness".

Notice how much more powerful- and accurate- it is to say of a friend who is notable for his kindness, for example, that he is "compassionate" rather than merely "nice". Both are one hundred percent true. But "nice" is general and non-specific, while "compassionate" captures the essence of the person. To describe him as "compassionate" is to speak to a listener with far more accuracy! That is what real testimony can be: finding the simple word that speaks to the essence of truth.

Brainstorm with your witness. What characterizations are needed in your case? Are there people who need to be described more thoughtfully, so as to capture their essence? Companies? Events? Places?

The "Five W's" Exercise

Ask your witness to think of an issue in the case that created some controversy and make a list of the people involved and the actions taken (or not taken). Now, consider the first person on the list and address the "who, what, where, when, and why" with regard to him and his actions. Characterize each of the "who's", then the "what's", then the "where's, etc.

It should look and sound something like this:

Example of a First Event: "A sales representative lost a big client account"

Who: "A sales representative and a client" (Now, characterize the people in a way that captures the truth about them.)

An "inexperienced sales representative" and a "very demanding" client.

What: "There was a disagreement with the sales representative." (Now, characterize both the disagreement and the sales representative.)

An "unnecessary" disagreement between a "very demanding" client and an "inexperienced" sales rep.

Go on to the "where", "when, and "why" characterizations, continuing the pattern.

• A witness may fear that the language he uses to speak truthfully about something will be unlike that selected by others. You should explain that several people might notice quite different aspects of a person (or a thing, a situation, and event) and thus speak quite differently of it. Yet all are being absolutely honest and truthful. This reality isn't in and of itself problematic. What is problematic is when a witness lacks confidence in his own truth. Encourage your witness to feel confident about whatever is true for him. It is his Truth. He can use his words.

• You may wish to tell your witnesses the parable of The Blind Men and the Elephant. It's a tale in which six blind men visit the palace of the Rajah and are given the opportunity to touch an elephant for the first time.

Here is the moment as told by author Lillian Quigley in her children's book of the same name:

"The first blind man put out his hand and touched the side of the elephant. "How smooth! An elephant is like a wall." The second blind man put out his hand and touched the trunk of the elephant. "How round! An elephant is like a snake." The third blind man put out his hand and touched the tusk of the elephant. "How sharp! An elephant is like a spear." The fourth blind man put out his hand and touched the leg of the elephant. "How tall! An elephant is like a tree." The fifth blind man reached out his hand and touched the ear of the elephant. "How wide! An elephant is like a fan." The sixth blind man put out his hand and touched the tail of the elephant. "How thin! An elephant is like a rope.""

To continue the tale, there ensues a violent argument, as each insists the others are fools, or worse, liars. Finally, the wise Rajah explains that to find the real truth they must consolidate the things they know. They must put their findings together to discern the true nature of an elephant. That, of course, is just what it can be like in litigation, as the different perspectives (all truthful) of several of your witnesses are assembled to complete an overall picture.

• Are there any elephants in your case waiting to be understood? If you simultaneously look at the different perspectives of different witnesses, does a pattern emerge? The only way to find out is to get those perspectives side by side. Put them up on a flip chart. Taken as whole cloth, what larger story might they tell? If you can look at that larger story together, you will be able to help your witness see how his testimony fits in. He will worry less. He will have greater trust in his own truth and be more confident about the words he selects because he understands that his testimony is only a part of a greater narrative.

Short Statements Tell it Best

• Good witnesses give short answers. Short answers are clear answers. Short answers are easy to understand. The subject comes first, then the verb, then the object. The sentences contain no more than one or two descriptive terms.

   Notice how the above section reads. The statements are written in the very style they espouse. It is not exciting reading, but it is clear and unambiguous. Your goal for your witness should be to have most of his testimony meet this standard. The judge and jury will appreciate it.

• In the handbook, *Hotseat*, the reader is instructed as follows:

   "Try as best you can to speak in short, simple sentences when answering questions in a testimony setting: Subject, verb, object - with only one or two characterizing (descriptive) words. Here's an example: Susan (subject) kissed (verb) Bob (object) passionately (descriptive). This simple style of speech will work best. It may sound awkward or boring to you, but your listeners will appreciate the clarity of your communication. You will make very few misstatements and the audience will not misunderstand you. Forcing yourself to speak in short sentences in this way will help you to organize your mind, too. You will have to focus upon how to describe specific things very clearly."

• Most experienced litigation attorneys have seen and heard (too many times!) deposition testimony that is characterized by rambling, confusing answers to what are often simple questions. It is as though the witness is thinking aloud, wandering up and down the aisles of his mental storehouse, narrating as he goes, and creating confusion instead of clarity.

• The lesson here is important. Long, complicated answers will simply not be remembered in their original form. Listeners will reduce them to short statements, perhaps even to short phrases, titles — sometimes even wordless images — in order to render them to a scale that can be comfortably kept in mind. You have no idea what short mental summaries might be created by listeners after hearing your witness produce a rambling compound-complex sentence. As noted earlier with regard to names, summary thoughts generated by listeners could be completely wrong. Inaccurate. Key elements may fall out of the message, lost on the cutting-room floor. The way to prevent this problem is to help the testifier learn to present key facts and ideas in short form with useful titles and names for each important element. If delivered in a compact package, the listeners will appreciate and remember the message.

• What follows are some exercises that can help your witness tune his ear to the length and clarity of her statements.

The "Dictation" Exercise

Ask your witness to answer some questions about the case as though he is dictating to a note-taker or secretary. It should sound something like this:

"Q. Mr. Anthony, can you tell the jury about your work?

A. "Certainly, I can period I am the Senior Vice President of Sales period My job is to get our product to market period I work with several vice presidents comma one for each region of the country comma in providing training and marketing resources to our sales representatives period"

(Incidentally, this is a good example of what we have long called a "one, two, three answer" to an open-ended question. It's got the maximum number of facts a single answer should contain [3]. It delivers them in separate statements. And, it delivers them in the order that is easiest to remember.)

As you can see, this exercise demands that a speaker listen to himself and monitor the structure of his statements. Most of us don't do this consciously unless we dicate a great deal. Consequently, many of us are lazy about sentence structure. Particularly, we are lazy about putting endings to our sentences! It usually doesn't take much of this type exchange for a long-winded witness to show marked improvement!

The "Run-on" Exercise

Help your witness improve his self-monitoring skills. Suggest that he answer your question, but prohibit the use of short statements. Insist that the entire answer be one long run-on sentence, with every clause joined to the next by a conjunction (a word that joins two clauses of a sentence) such as "and", "but", "if", or "so", etc.. It should sound something like this:

Q. "Mr. Anthony, can you tell the jury about your work?

A. "Certainly I can so I am the Senior Vice President of Sales and my job is to get our product to market so I work with several vice presidents and one for each region of the country and we're providing training and marketing resources for our sales representatives and…"

The answer can sound hilarious after only a few moments, but the lesson is nevertheless learned. Do a couple of rounds of these two exercises, alternating dictation-style answers with run-on answers to increase your witness' sensitivity to the length and structure of his statements.

Occasionally we have issued a written tongue-in-cheek "Conjunction Injunction" to a witness who over-uses connecting words like "but", "and" and "so"! We've handed one to the occasional attorney, too…

The "You Know" Exercise

Another big problem is frequent use of the space-filler "you know" in witness responses. You will hear many witnesses use "you know", "like", and "uh" as conjunctions! If your witness has this habit, get him to overuse the offending words intentionally as the only allowed joining term in his answer. This will increase his sensitivity to it. We have seen and heard many speakers abandon such terms after only one or two rounds of the "you know", or "you know, and" exercise!

Note that it is called the "You Know" exercise, but it should focus on whatever filler term your witness is using! If it's "and, uh", then do an "And, Uh" exercise.

The "You Know" exercise should sound something like this:

Q. "Mr. Anthony, can you tell the jury about your work?"

A. "Certainly I can you know I am the Senior Vice President of Sales you know and my job is to get our product to market you know and I work with several vice presidents you know one for each region of the country you know in providing training and marketing resources for you know our sales representatives."

Please take the time and trouble to do this if you have a witness with one of these annoying speech habits. Gap-filling words and phrases tend to appear more and more frequently in speech as people get more anxious. Most witnesses will be anxious at least some of the time during their testimony. If he's got an issue with this, help him. It is worth the effort!

• Once your witness is thinking about communicating his truth in short, well-structured statements, give him some opportunities to do so. Ask him to summarize in just such statements the essence of events, situations, or issues with regard to your case. Listen carefully and challenge him to get the facts clear and accurate. He will have been thinking about the words that make the most sense for him, the characterizations that are important to help him correctly express his perspective. Now it is time to put them together.

• Listen thoughtfully, with the ear of a juror. You can't tell your witness what the truth is, but you can tell him how he's doing at speaking the truth coherently. If he is pushed to communicate with precision in these exchanges with you, he will better learn to attend to clarity and accuracy. He will naturally recall terms that get him to his goal of delivering testimony with power and confidence. It will be his truth, well said.

Precise Limits

• Let's talk about a common error: a witness thinks he knows something when in fact he doesn't. In the handbook *Hotseat*, readers learn this:

"Did you know that many of us say things as truth to others in ordinary conversation that we could never "swear to"? Our spoken exchanges with friends or family often include the communication of beliefs, judgments, assumptions, guesses, theories, gossip, unverified stories from others, and things we get from the newspapers or television- all presented as truth. Unfortunately, none of those things meets the strict test of truth. Why? Because we do not actually know these things. We may believe them or treat them as truth, but that is not the same.

For you to have full confidence that something about which you speak is true, you usually have to be the original source of the information. You saw it. You felt it. You heard it. You did it. You said it. Otherwise, it's just something you heard about or read about or (worst) guessed."

• Go through your witness' factual recitations with a fine-toothed comb, helping him understand the strict test he must apply to that about which he will testify. You don't want him to get caught up and embarrassed during his testimony over some small thing that he too casually assumes to be true, but which really doesn't deserve the status of truth because it is inferred it rather than experienced. Help him to become sensitive to this important distinction.

• Just as a witness should work on how to speak clearly and confidently to what he knows, he should speak just as clearly and confidently to what he does not know. Too many witnesses get worried because they don't command every single detail of a situation or they don't understand all the technical issues in a case. The secret to success here is for a witness to remain comfortable with that over which he is master and not feel weakened merely because his mastery has limits.

The "You Don't Even Know" Exercise

Get into cross-examining mode and then ask your witness – completely out of the blue – almost any question about a simple fact the witness surely knows, then challenge him for not knowing something else. It should sound something like this:

Q. "What is your birth date?

A. "April 17, 1973"

Q. "You know that you were born on April 17, 1973, but you don't even know my birthday, do you?"

A. "You're absolutely correct about that. I do know mine and I don't know yours."

The point here is to give your witness a chance to laugh at the silliness of implying that he must know one thing in order to be confident that he knows another! But, let's move it closer to home.

Ask your witness some easy question with regard to your case, then immediately follow with a "you don't even know" question. It ought to sound like this:

Q. "Where were you and what were you doing at the time of the accident?"

A. "I was walking South on 7th Street. I was on my way to work."

Q. "What, if any, vehicles passed you at that time?"

A. "I am not sure. The only ones I remember are the truck and the mini-van that were in the collision."

Q. "You say you remember all that, but you don't even know what other vehicles passed you, do you?"

A. "You're right. I didn't really pay attention to vehicles until I saw those two getting ready to collide!"

Do some variation of this exercise at least a couple of times, so that your witness can have the good feeling of agreeing that he doesn't know everything, and at the same time remain confident in what he does know.

• **The Rule of Knowledge**: You can't know something that is un-knowable. You don't have real knowledge of what happened in the living room when you were in the kitchen. It's impossible. You can't know what would have happened if your life had been different. It's impossible. And, importantly, you can't speak to the currents of thought and feeling inside any person but yourself. That, too, is impossible. Teach this rule to your witness. Once you have explained the rule, you can simply invoke it by the use of its name. It is portable and capacious.

• One of the biggest pitfalls for witnesses is what psychologists call "mind-reading". Mind-reading is what we are doing when we talk as though we know what someone is thinking or feeling. Here is the most important place where the Rule of Knowledge applies.

• Your witness can assume, or guess, or theorize- but she cannot truly know the thoughts of another. In fact, she cannot know the thoughts of another person even if that person tells her about the thoughts. She only knows what the person said about his thoughts; she still doesn't know the thoughts themselves.

The "How did Bob Feel About That?" Exercise

Do this exercise: Consider a person involved in the case about whom your witness may be questioned. Then ask your witness questions that invite comment upon that person's state of mind, opinions, or feelings. It should sound like this:

Q. "So, Bob Johnson was there, too?"

A. "Yes, Sir. Bob was there."

Q. "How did Bob feel about what was going on?"

A. "I don't know what Bob felt. I can only tell you what he did."

Some question variations: "Bob was comfortable with that, wasn't he?" "What kind of mood was Bob in that day?" "Bob didn't like that plan, did he?" "Bob trusts you, doesn't he?" etc. These should all draw accurate answers where the witness confidently asserts that he doesn't (and can't) know about Bob's feelings. Importantly, neither should he theorize about Bob's feelings based on observing his actions. That too can only be a guess, not the truth.

Emails and other documents also must "speak for themselves". The Rule of Knowledge applies here, too. It is inappropriate (and inaccurate) to try to say what the writer "means" by an email. Give your witness opportunities to answer questions about the contents of any documents about which he may be questioned. He will be better armed for testimony if he knows how to stick to the truth of a document: It means only what it says, unless he is the one who wrote it.

Do the following exercise with your witness so that he can practice applying the Rule of Knowledge to a document. As always, do several variations so that the witness can begin to recognize the common thread that joins "mind reading" questions.

The "What did Bob Mean?" Exercise

Q. "Let's look at this email from Bob Johnson. He says here, '…and all of our team will attend the meeting.' Do you see that?

A. "Yes, Sir."

Q. "What this means is that he is going to bring everyone who was working on that project to the meeting. Isn't that correct?"

A. "I don't know what he was thinking, so I don't know what he meant. I only know what it says here."

Some variations: "What he's saying here is that everyone is coming. Right?" "This is letting you know what he is planning. Isn't that correct?" "He's telling you that this is important to him, isn't he?"

Help your witness work to be very clear on this topic. He should express precise limits to his knowledge concerning the thoughts and actions - and writings - of others. It will enable him to stick more exactly to the truth. He will be a credible and trustworthy testifier.

The Whole Truth: Background and Context

• In the handbook *Hotseat,* the reader is introduced to the following important concept:

"When another person tells us about something that happened to him, our sense of the meaning of that event is shaped by what we already know about that person and the circumstances in which the event happened. Knowing the background and context of an event helps us understand the whole truth about that event."

• "Background", as we use it here, means "history". Often there are key elements of your case that can only be correctly understood when set against the factual backdrop of a unique history. You will need to discuss this topic with your witness and help him be alert to questions he may be asked with regard to those key elements. The questioner may not address the history at all, so the witness - in order to fulfill his oath to testify to the whole truth - will need to include the historical reference with his answer. To do otherwise risks inaccuracy and misunderstanding.

• Remember the parable of "The Boy Who Cried 'Wolf'"? Tell this story to your witness as an example of the need for background in order to understand a situation:

"The Boy Who Cried Wolf" is an old folk tale about a young shepherd boy who became old enough to take his turn to guard the flock from predators. On his first night, he decided to tease the older shepherds by crying out,

"Wolf!" as loudly as he could. This caused the shepherds to leave their beds and come running to his aid, believing that he needed help to keep the wolf away from their sheep. When they realized that it was a false alarm, they were upset with him and scolded him. But, he thought it was a great joke! He did it the next night and the next, making the other shepherds angrier and angrier. On the fourth night the boy was on watch and a real wolf came hunting. The boy cried "Wolf!" at the top of his voice, but the jaded shepherds in the camp thought he was just teasing again and this time ignored him. The consequences were catastrophic.

• Imagine the Supervising Shepherd being deposed some time after that terrible night. Notice that he hasn't learned to include the necessary background with his answer:

Q. "So, when young Billy cried "Wolf!", you didn't go and help him, did you?"

A. "No, Sir, I didn't."

Q. "You left him out there, didn't you? Just stayed in your warm bed, isn't that right?"

A. "Like I said, I didn't go."

Now, let's have the Supervising Shepherd make reference in his answers to the historical background. Notice how different this sounds when he points his answer towards the whole truth:

Q. "So, when young Billy cried "Wolf!" you didn't go and help him, did you?"

A. "That's right. Because of what happened before, we decided to not go."

Q. "You left him out there, didn't you? Just stayed in your warm bed, isn't that right?"

A. "Yes, Sir. It's sad, but we were trying to teach him an important lesson."

• Just as knowledge of the background of the case can be helpful to fact finders, so too can the knowledge of the personal background of the witness. In everyday life, it is by understanding someone's history that we make sense of his attitudes and behavior. Providing this same information can make a great deal of difference in the sometimes too-narrow universe of a lawsuit, helping a jury understand choices the witness made.

The "Life History" Exercise

Take an hour or two or so to learn about your witness' life.

You should try to do it as a structured interview, asking about discreet periods in his life and then asking what major events happened in that period.

You should be interested in births, deaths, accidents, and moves from one place to another. You should learn what his parents' occupations were, major events for his parents that occurred while he was a child, memorable vacations, and about his best friends, etc.

You are likely to learn about events in his life that will help you understand him. This feeling of "knowing him" will improve your communication with him. You are also likely to learn things that inform you more deeply about his views of your case and his role in it. As one lawyer put it, "That's where the gold is!"

Your interview should sound something like this:

Q. "Tell me a little about your parents. Where are they from, what were their occupations, and where did they live when you were born?

A. "I was born on a mountaintop in Tennessee...."

Q. "Now I want to ask you about several periods in your life and I'd like you to tell me the key facts about that period. Here's the kind of thing I'd like to know: I'm interested in births, deaths, moves, life changes for you, your parents, or other family members, and any key events you remember from that period. I want to know that about each period.

Q. "Now tell me about your elementary school years- trying to include the same key information.

Then Adolescence: Junior High and High School
Early Adulthood: First job and/or college experiences
Subsequent Employment and/or Educational Experiences
Marriage or relationships w significant others

• Obviously, exploring your witness' life is not meant to be an exhaustive process, nor is it counseling. It is getting to know someone well enough to understand who they are and how they come to be in the witness chair. Don't forget to ask follow-up questions! Learn more about that trip to Mexico when he was six years old, or why he quit playing baseball in high school.

• For a variety of reasons, many attorneys resist the suggestion to explore their witness' personal history. Amazingly, the ones who resist the most will often later reverse themselves, declaring that this was the one of the most valuable things they did in preparing their witness for testimony.

• One final suggestion with regard to background – and perhaps the hardest: Consider taking time to tell the witness about yourself in somewhat the same style as above. Tell him what kind of little kid you were. Then, with your own life story, grow yourself up before his eyes into the lawyer he will be relying upon during his testimony. He will then have that feeling of "knowing" you. The result will be better rapport. He will trust you more.

Context

• We have just covered two useful ways to teach the truth about the people, objects, and events in a case. The first is to use accurate names and descriptive words that capture the essence of the thing named. The second is to give useful background information, usually in a narrative that teaches the listener how to think about the thing against the backdrop of history. We shall now discuss a third. That is to provide adequate context information; to teach about other people, objects, or events - usually existing concurrently - that affect the thing in question and that help to explain it. You and your witness may need to think and talk a lot about context.

• Context is not merely color and flavor for your story. Sometimes you will find that the context IS the story, and the event only a small element. Learn to ask for contextual information. You may very well discover other key dynamics that were at play during key events. There may be forces you will understand to be relevant that the witness doesn't recognize as important, and thus won't think to tell you about unless you ask. You've got to initiate the exploration and help the witness consider how things fit together. Contemplating these matters will help him speak to the whole truth when testifying.

• In the handbook *Hotseat*, the reader learns the following:

"Remember, as people listen to you speak in response to a specific question, they are often putting together a bigger picture. They are inserting assumptions, making guesses, coming up with intuitive judgments about the

complete truth. You make this much easier for them when you give them accurate context information to use in the process. You are helping them get to the whole truth.

Here are some examples of (personal) context information that can often help listeners learn the whole truth from your testimony:

Your health at the time in question.
Your family's health and circumstances.
Your mood and mindset at the time.
What you had been doing just before the time in question.
What you did just after that time.
What else is going on in proximity to you.
What other people were nearby, involved or not.
What was going on in the neighborhood, town, state, nation, world at the time."

• You may profit from going through the above list with your witness.

The "Truth Circle" Exercise

Draw some circles on a note pad or flip chart. In the center circle, put the event or issue in question. What important things need to be understood by the judge and jury about the immediate time and place and topic? What must be addressed as though from that spot? Then go to the next circle out. What important things about the surrounding milieu need to be understood by judge and jury? In other words, what must be explained that is outside the event, but relevant to it? Then go to the next circle, the larger context of the witness' work and life, and go through the same process.

Example: Imagine a lawsuit about an accident involving a worker in a factory where your witness is employed. Your witness is being blamed for creating the conditions that caused the accident to happen.

The Truth Circle should include this:

Outer Circle - Life Context
Facts that teach about who your witness is; what he believes; how he does things.

Middle Circle - Indirect Context
Facts that that teach about the factory, the company, the witness' career, co-workers

Inner Circle – Immediate Context
Facts that immediately surround the event; who, what, when, where

• A useful skill for a witness to acquire is to be able to introduce an answer to a question before actually delivering it. In the handbook *Hotseat* readers learn this:

"The next time you watch or listen to the news, pay attention to the way reporters work to put key context information into the front end of stories. Usually it's the intro that gives context and thus explains why the story is of interest.

Compare these two introductions:

Number 1: "In our next story, A Person walks Half a Mile to Borrow a Phone"

Huh? Who cares? Why should I be interested in this story? But, let's look at the second version which contains some provocative context information.

Number 2: "In our next story, A Blind Child Whose Mother is Ill Walks Half a Mile Cross-Country to Call 911."

Wow! That context information makes the story nearly irresistible, doesn't it? You want to know what happened! Everyone does!

The objective fact that a person walked half a mile remains the same objective fact, of course. But that fact gets its real meaning from the context, the related facts which explain why it matters. Importantly, receiving the context information first helps the listener absorb and understand the complete picture. Otherwise, the risk of misunderstanding is increased.

Testifiers think a lot about context and background facts and how to say them clearly and concisely. They also learn to "introduce" their answers to questions, not unlike the way a newscaster does."

• More than once in any given deposition, or in testimony at trial, a question on an important point will demand a contextualized answer in order to be adequately answered. In other words, the answer is only the whole truth if it has all of its parts. Otherwise, it is less than whole, less than true. The best way for a witness to provide such answers is to have thought about it earlier.

• Discussing context with you and thinking aloud about how to express it clearly will help the witness clarify his thinking AND his expression of that thinking. Keep talking with him about it until he can tell you about it in several different ways, always remembering to include the key elements of context that characterize the fact in question.

Obviously, this will not be particularly hard to do in direct testimony or when asked open-ended questions. It is somewhat more difficult with closed-end questions.

Here's an example of a simple closed-end question:

Q: "…and you were driving 70 miles an hour that night, weren't you?"

A. "Yes, Sir"

Here's an example of an introduced answer to the above question. An introduced answer prepares the listener's ear for the necessary context information.

A. "Yes, I was so worried about my mother that I drove as fast as I could!"

Notice how the above answer says, "There is important context information the listener ought to have!", but doesn't attempt to cram it all into the response? This type answer doesn't beg a follow-up question. It demands it. A questioner almost has to follow-up! To fail to do so would be to upset the listener. A certain dramatic tension has been established and it has to be resolved.

• Context information shouldn't be gratuitously stuffed into every response your witness makes. It will be seen as non-responsive and draw an objection from questioning counsel. Doing it repeatedly will only draw a rebuke from a judge and contempt from a jury. This type answer should be reserved for matters of greater weight than ordinary.

• You and your witness should discuss what topics need to be answered in full context in order for him to meet his responsibility to testify to the whole truth. He should strive to do just that when those matters come up, and refrain from doing so elsewhere.

Nothing But the Truth: Defending Against Mischaracterization and Inaccuracy

• In the handbook, *Hotseat*, the reader learns this important lesson:

"The words you speak in the role of testifier should meet the strict test of being nothing but the truth. If there is controversy, though, your statements are likely to be challenged. You will probably have to defend and explain your view of things. You may also need to react honestly and truthfully to different or opposing views. Because of this, you frequently have to spend more energy preparing for questioning by skeptical or opposing parties than for telling your story directly. Importantly, answering questions from someone with an opposing position - defending your truth - requires that you have a good knowledge of other views of things. Depending upon your role in the story, you may need to be able to speak with the same thoughtfulness and clarity you will have brought to speaking your own truth to both the criticisms of your testimony and any contradictory testimony of others. There could be a lot of thinking to do."

• Being deposed or cross-examined can be an excruciating experience for a witness. Witnesses who were committed to honesty and candor under oath, and are trying their best to deliver, have time and again been eviscerated by skillful examiners. It is not the facts themselves that are the problem, nor the veracity of the witness. It is the harsh reality of the legal contest, where the winning instrument of play is as often the skillfully crafted question as the honestly delivered answer.

• Your energies, like that of your witness will thus need to be directed as much or more to preparing for the questions as for the answers. Why? Because the rules of adverse examination favor the questioner. You can help your witness gain a significant measure of control by first helping him understand some rules.

• In *Hotseat*, the reader sees this:

> *"In general, the rules for a testifier in a question-answer situation are these:*
>
> *You must speak only the truth.*
> *You should not refuse to answer a question (unless it would be legally improper to answer).*
> *The questioner decides what topics will be covered and in what order.*
> *The questioner decides how to structure the questions.*
> *The questioner decides what terms and characterizations to use in the questions.*
> *The questioner decides what, if any, propositions are built into the questions."*

• Your witness will need you to teach him how to deal with challenging questions. In order to deal with them, he has to first learn how to listen to them. We know that frequently people do not listen to the entirety of a question. They seem to listen for the general subject of the question, then reply intuitively to what they judge to be the thrust of it, rather than composing an answer that matches the specifics of the inquiry. In ordinary conversation, this type of approximated response is often accepted as satisfactory.

For example: A polite, "How's your Mama?" to a friend might elicit a story about the friend's Mama having surgery. But, it also might get the questioner a story about Mama's recent argument with a neighbor, or about Mama's new hobby, etc. The questioner may or may not follow up. After all, it's just conversation. Giving testimony, your witness must understand, is NOT just conversation.

The "Repeat the Question" Exercise

Ask your witness a series of questions about anything: his job, sports, the weather. Start with short questions, move to lengthier ones, then to compound, and finally to compound-complex questions. For the purposes of this first exercise, make the questions closed-ended and factually correct. Don't put any tricky references or mischaracterizations in, as that will add unnecessary complexity to this exercise. (You can do that later!) For now, make the questions all straightforward "yes-no" questions.

Tell your witness you don't want a question answered until after he repeats it back to you verbatim. Only then may he answer the question. Make a game of it at first by – for example - inserting a small amount of data into a simple question to make it fun and more challenging. (unfamiliar names, sports scores, phone numbers, scientific terms).

It should sound something like this:

Q. "Did you see the Reds' game last night?"

A. "Did (I) see the Reds' game last night?" "Yes."

Q. "Did you see that the Reds' won by a score of 9 to 4?"

A. "Did (I) see that the Reds' won by a score of 9 to 4?' "Yes."

Q. "Did you see that the Reds' also had 13 hits and only 1 error?"

A. "Did (I) see that the Reds' also had 13 hits and only 1 error?" "No, I didn't notice that."

Let's jump a few steps down the line:

Q. "Did you realize that, because the second baseman had a sore left shoulder, they were playing him closer to the bag, and that was the reason he couldn't get to the line drive that Lopez hit into short center field in the 8th inning?"

A. "Huh? Can you break that down?"

Now we are getting somewhere! This exercise has more to it than just getting witnesses to listen carefully. It also can show the difficulty of holding a compound-complex question clearly in mind so as to answer it. For now, you only want to accomplish one simple thing with this exercise. That is to help your witness recognize that "Huh?" feeling.

• Here's an important rule of thumb: If a witness cannot hold the question and all its parts clearly in mind, he should not be expected to answer it. More importantly, he usually should not attempt to answer it, even if he thinks he has the "gist" of it. The chance of misunderstanding the question is very high in this scenario, and he should proceed carefully if he is to fulfill his duty to the truth.

• We'll look at too-long questions a little more closely in a later section and and we'll discuss the tools with which your witness can deal with them. For now, let's stay focused on how you can help him tune his ear to the content and style of questions.

• You will want to stress to your witnesses that these listening exercises matter a great deal because the best testifiers are also the best listeners. The best testifiers understand that a witness can exert a significant amount of control over the nature and style of questions she must answer. But, it all starts with paying careful attention to the questions!

- It is important for witnesses to know that they don't have to accept a question that is too long, or is confusing, or which contains words the witness doesn't understand. They should not attempt an answer. They should politely challenge the question. Consider the following exercise.

- After helping your witness get better at listening carefully enough to questions that he can repeat them word-for-word, then you want to help him sensitize his ear to the problem elements that can appear in questions. You'll also want to teach him what to do when he detects such elements.

The "Question the Question" Exercise

Ask your witness some questions in adverse-questioner mode. The questions can be of any style, but you should include within the question one or more of the common problem elements: an inappropriate or inaccurate factual reference, an inaccurate or offensive characterization, an unwarranted conclusion, an unacceptable assumption, etc.

Then, give your witness the chance to practice making a graceful and polite challenge to the question. How? By asking a question about the question.

It should sound something like this:

Q.: "Mr. Jones, when your company decided to rush this cheap machine into the marketplace, they were putting profit ahead of safety, weren't they?"

A. "Excuse me, I'm not sure I understand the question. Can you ask it again?" (The old stand-by: Ask to have the question repeated. Maybe the questioner will take at least part the problem out. But, don't bank on it! This mechanism mostly just tells the questioner that the problem has been noticed by the deponent.)

A. "I'm sorry, but I'm not sure what you mean by "rush to the marketplace"? (This mechanism usually forces the questioner to consider defining the term in a second and different question. No matter though, the deponent now has a measure of control.)

A. "Excuse me, could you tell me what you mean when you say we "rushed a cheap machine into the marketplace"? (This directly requests an explanation of the word choice. The questioner has to deliver now, or, as most do, he will move to a different question. In either event, the deponent has controlled the moment.)

There are a number of ways your witness can "question the question", but make sure you teach him this important rule: Question the question, NOT the questioner. Say, "I don't understand what you mean." Rather than, "I don't understand you." The latter personalizes the exchange and connects the quality of the question to the quality of the person. This can antagonize some questioners. That is an unnecessary complexity.

The "Detect-and-Correct" Exercise

Have a conversation with your witness in which you speak to her only by asking leading questions that contain assumptions. Tell her she should listen for even the smallest inaccuracies in the questions and answer by correcting the inaccuracy. Give her a chance to listen to and respond to them in whatever method comes naturally. The goal is for her to detect erroneous assumptions and insert correct statements in her response.

It should sound something like this (Just pick an ordinary topic, such as her car, and start making guesses which you then embed in a leading question. You will find this easy and fun.):

Q. "Your car is a 2008 Toyota Camry, isn't it?" (A wild guess! You've never seen her car! Press on!)

A. "No, Sir, it's a Tahoe."

Q. "Your Tahoe is green and has an oil leak, isn't that true?"

A. "No, Sir, it's white and there is nothing wrong with it."

Q. "You are crazy about your car, aren't you?"

A. "Well, Sir, I sure like my Tahoe a lot."

Q. "And you'll never want any other kind of car, will you?"

A. "Not true, Sir. I might get a sports car someday."

In our example, this witness very comfortably pushes back on inaccurate statements offered as facts. She shows pretty refined listening skills, too, as she detects-and-corrects the overstated "…crazy about your car…" to "…I sure like my Tahoe…"

- You should stress to her that, when under oath, she should not go along with the use of any terms in a leading question with which she does not 100% agree. She should disagree with them and politely submit different language in the same kind of natural correcting response that she uses here.

It is in this "pushing-back" component of testimony where politeness on the part of a witness really matters. Notice in the example, that our witness addresses the attorney as "Sir" in every answer. Doing it this way in the exercise helps her train herself to contradict a questioner (if she must) in a courteous manner. It might sound a bit formal, but it is always socially acceptable to be *too* polite to an adversary. Being insufficiently polite, on the other hand, is risky. Encourage all your witnesses to make any social errors, if such errors occur at all, in the direction of excessive attention to courtesy. Too much politeness is always better than too little.

After you have done the Detect-and-Correct exercise with a witness, help her recognize the implications of what she has done. She listened to a question and found that it contained an erroneous assumption. She rejected the question as originally formed and submitted a response that essentially corrected the error. It is by doing just that - auditing the question and then correcting it in the response – that witnesses can take a measure of control and better defend their sense of the truth.

Stress to your witness that she need not feel powerless when being questioned by an opposing attorney. Her power is born from two well-established legal realities: (1) The witness has the right to an answerable question and (2) the witness has the right to give complete answers. Most attorneys and witnesses focus on the latter. But that is only half of the battle.

It is assuring themselves answerable questions that witnesses usually must learn from the beginning, with cumulative skill building lessons such as the ones taught here. The good news is that it doesn't take long for most people to catch on to these ideas. Once they attain some mastery over the questions, they will become much more effective with the answers.

• What are the qualities of an answerable question? From the layman's perspective, they are these:

> An answerable question is audible and delivered at a pace the witness can follow.
> An answerable question is one the witness can hold in mind. It is not too long.
> An answerable question is one that is comprehensible. It is not illogical.
> An answerable question is one that is grammatically correct in its structure.
> An answerable question in one that is free of inaccurate or incorrect assumptions.
> An answerable question does not oblige a witness to agree to factual errors or inaccurate characterizations.
> An answerable question does not oblige a witness to agree to a half-truth.

• Well-prepared witnesses notice when a question has any of the above flaws and usually don't attempt to answer the as-asked question. Your witness can learn to do this, too.

• One fundamental issue: Make sure your witness can actually hear the questions. Does your witness have any trouble with hearing? If so, have a plan to deal with it. Most court-reporting services can provide listener-assist headphones. If the questioning attorneys speak in a low voice or makes rambling, soft-spoken introductions to questions, be ready to intervene. Your witness should not have to work extra hard to hear a question! The burden is already heavy enough.

• If the questioning pace is too fast, your witness will need to know that he can ask the questioner to slow down. Sometimes the questioning attorney simply speaks at a rapid rate, and the questions themselves are hard to follow. If that's the case, your witness should know how to say something like this: "I want to make sure I understand your question, but you are speaking a bit too fast for me. Would you please slow down?" Now you have it in the record. You should intervene in your witness' behalf if it happens again.

• The other problem related to pace is when one question rushes in so quickly behind another that the witness has no time to gather himself, to have a sip of water, or take a breath. Once again, he should know that he can say something about it. Something like, "Give me a moment, please. I want to clear my mind so that I can listen to your next question."

The goal is for your witness to testify to the truth. If a question is rushed at him while he is still collecting his thoughts from the question preceding, he may misunderstand and respond in a way that is confusing or incorrect. He's not asking for special treatment, he's asking to be given the opportunity to fulfill his oath.

• If questions are too long, your witness may have trouble keeping clear on what is being asked. As discussed earlier with regard to the "Repeat the Question" exercise, he should always be able to recite a question back word-for-word. If he can't do so, it is often because the question is simply too long. If it is too long to remember, it will be of necessity reduced to summary thought in the witness' brain. The risk of miscommunication with the questioner then becomes very real.

The "System Overload" Exercise

The witness will come to recognize that unpleasant feeling which occurs when the question has become too long to follow. It will be as though his brain has gone into "system overload". Give him a chance to practice the following techniques for managing the situation. Remember, it is less likely that he learns these skills by you merely telling him how to utilize them. He should be allowed to actually do it - and do it more than once - in order to internalize the skills.

Do a few repeats of too-long questions with your witness so that he can have the feeling of detecting a system overload and then either rejecting the question or selecting only part of it to comment upon. It should sound something like the sequence below.

Let's go back to the long question about baseball that we used in the "Get the Question" exercise:

Q. "Did you realize that, because the second baseman had a sore left shoulder, they were playing him closer to the bag, and that was the reason he couldn't get to the line drive that Lopez hit into short center field in the 8th inning?"

A. "Huh?"

What else might the witness have done?

Detect and Reject

Your witness could have simply detected that the question was too long, that he was feeling overloaded, and then politely rejected it as unanswerable in that form. It might sound something like this:

Q. "Did you realize that, because the second baseman had a sore left shoulder, they were playing him closer to the bag, and that was the reason he couldn't get to the line drive that Lopez hit into short center field?"

A. "I'm sorry, the question was really long. Can you re-phrase it?"

Detect and Select

Another choice is for your witness to detect that the question is too long to keep clearly in mind and simply select a single part of the question to talk about. This is not (in the legal sense) a "responsive answer", but it is a natural and courteous reply that signals to the questioner that he will have to revisit the matter. A detect-and-select response might sound something like this:

Q. "Did you realize that, because the second baseman had a sore left shoulder, they were playing him closer to the bag, and that was the reason he couldn't get to the line drive that Lopez hit into short center field?"

A. "I did know that the second baseman had been injured. But, what was the rest of the question?"

The second version submitted by the questioner will probably be shorter and more streamlined. If the questioner persists with the original wording, and the witness is still uncomfortable about its clear meaning, then he should politely reject the question.

As you and your witness get more comfortable working together, you can switch from practicing these techniques using generic material to using material that is related to your case. You will both like the rewards of such work.

• Forced-choice questions are another device that often stymies witnesses who have not been taught how to handle them. In *Hotseat*, the reader learns this:

"Forced-choice questions are questions that are designed to limit the options of the person answering. As the name implies, you have to make a decision, you are forced to choose, usually between two positions. Forced-choice questions have great utility in the worlds of science and mathematics and philosophy. For the same reasons, they also have some utility in testing the truth of a statement or the strength of a position, as they may compel clear thought AND clear speech in both the person asking and the person answering. A proposition is positioned as a question and you must accept or reject it, agree or disagree. That seems okay, doesn't it? But, what happens in the real world?

What happens is that testifiers get asked these yes/no questions and just don't believe they can really be answered with a simple yes or no. Sometimes they get asked these questions and think the answer is something close to yes, or close to no, but not always- not all the time. They don't know what to do. But, you will know what to do. You will understand that you should not answer, "Yes." if the answer should actually be "Most of the time-yes". Your assignment is to answer accurately. Be very clear on the essential premise: "Yes", and "Most of the time-yes" are different. That is the whole truth and nothing but the truth.

Many times, you just can't answer a question with a simple yes/no or agree/disagree. If that is the case, you should say so - because that is the truth. Do not be afraid that you will be seen as impolite or difficult. If you are sincerely trying to get it right, your efforts will be appreciated and understood by most listeners."

• Explore the following material with your witness. It will help him internalize a valuable concept that all testifiers should understand.

The "Three Dimensions of Yes and No"

When someone asserts a yes/no or agree/disagree proposition with us, we have a wide range of choices available to help us make an accurate response. Generally, we have three dimensions of the affirmative and three dimensions of the negative.

Absolute Yes and No: The central dimension, and the "choice" typically being "forced" by a questioner is that of the absolute affirmative or absolute negative with regard to the "true-ness" of a posited objective fact. This is usually stated flatly as "Yes" or "No" and applies itself best to observable, verifiable realities. To most listeners this means "X" or "O", the switch is "off" or it is "on", the room is either light or it is dark. No exception. Period.

Once asserted, an absolute can then be used to fence a witness in, to further limit his testimony. For that reason the absolute response is coveted by many attorneys, and they will work long and late constructing questions designed to elicit it. But, too often, witnesses, not knowing what to do with the question, will answer in the absolute when it just isn't true. The attorney gets his prize, but it is undeserved. The witness is trapped by the demands of the question, not by the proposition asserted.

Limited Yes and No: The reality is that the answer to most such questions is something in-between the full affirmative and the full negative, and usually not even squarely in-between. That is our second dimension, an affirmative or negative response that must be limited in some way, defined, placed on a continuum.

What you have asserted, Mr. Attorney, is true, but only in a certain way.

Amplified Yes and No: Finally, there is the third dimension; an interesting one, too. Some proportion of forced-choice questions are designed, not merely to establish a fact, but to establish moral leverage ("You believe that people should be honest with each other, don't you?") with a witness. Or they are intended as pseudo-logical traps, baited and set in anticipation of a later inquiry. They can be tossed out as oh-by-the-way questions ("Before we start on this next topic- you agree that water is wet, don't you?") that are dripping with danger, should the witness hesitate even a moment in the answering. You will want your witness to know how to handle such questions.

Here are some examples of the former, some limited affirmatives, each placing the limitation in a slightly different spot on a continuum. These are "I agree" answers.

- Occasionally that's true
- Sometimes that's the case
- That's often how it is
- Correct, it's typically that way
- The majority of the time, right
- Almost always, that's correct
- Yes, that's accurate

Compare those examples to these "I don't agree" limited negatives:

- That's not a typical situation
- It's not usually that way
- That's hardly ever true
- That's an extremely rare scenario

- I've never heard of that
- No, that's not accurate

Ask your witness some questions in a forced-choice format, relevant to your case or not, and give him the opportunity to work on precisely limited affirmative and negative responses. There are countless ways to say these things, so let him find his own language, assuring only that it communicates the limitation clearly. The power of this type of answer lies, of course, in its pinpoint accuracy. It allows a witness to stick tightly to the truth, agreeing or disagreeing with general propositions without giving up the important exceptions.

• Do not think that merely explaining this concept will guarantee that your witness remembers how to do it. Most of us are lazy about generalizations in our everyday conversation and have to stretch in order to achieve precision. Give your witness the chance to stretch in this way, to practice this important skill of the disciplined truth-teller.

Now let's look at some examples of the amplified affirmative:

- I agree
- I think that is quite accurate
- That is certainly correct
- I believe you are right on that one
- That is exactly the case
- I absolutely concur with that
- I agree wholeheartedly
- That is absolutely, entirely, completely correct!

In the above series of examples, the tone is one of endorsement, as the witness takes a question like "I want a yes or no answer, Mr. Smith. You weren't prepared at all for that accident, were you?" and turns the reply - from what the questioning law-yer may have been hoping for, a sheepish-sounding admission - into an affirmative statement. The answer flows out powerfully because the witness knows how he feels on the topic and believes the most fully truthful answer to the question isn't merely an affirmative response, it is an affirmative response amplified by his agreement on the matter. It is dimensional, and includes both the fact and the feeling: the whole truth.

Some questions are painted in moral tones, and can have the effect of making a witness sound as though she is being forced to agree that a certain moral value is desirable. Here's our example from earlier: "You believe that people should be honest with each other, don't you?" Many witnesses will recognize intuitively that this question is probably intended to set them up for something. As a consequence, they may become defensive and might even be tempted to somehow evade the question, not because they don't agree with the value of honesty, but because they smell the proverbial rat behind the inquiry.

• Speak to what matters most, first. That means encourage your witness to endorse this value, because the truth is that she believes in it, and worry about that later question when and if it actually comes. She can take this moral-value question, answer it in the endorsing style that will feel honest and complete to her, and not feel dirtied by the hint of menace behind it. She should take first things first. How might all that sound?

Q. "You believe that people should be honest with each other, don't you?"

• Yes, Sir, I do
•   I certainly do
•   Of course I believe in honesty

66

- You bet, it's very important to be honest
- I think it's the key to success in life!
- I don't just believe in it- I teach it to my employees!

• Notice how the endorsement makes the response into a positive statement about her character. Much of the time, you and your witness will know a question like this is coming and she won't be afraid of whatever is to follow. But, whether or not she knows what is being foreshadowed by such a question, she should not let the questioner have moral high ground he doesn't deserve. He's not the only one who believes in honesty, as your witness has just honestly noted.

Let's look at some examples of the amplified negative form of a response.

Q. "You agree, don't you, that a supervisor should always be frank and tell an employee if that supervisor has concerns about the employee's work?"

- I disagree
- I think that is incorrect
- I don't believe it is that way at all
- That is simply not the case
- I absolutely disagree
- That could not be more wrong
- That is entirely and completely wrong

• By the use of an answering style designed to transform a rigid yes/no answer into a whole-truth statement, much of the sting is taken from forced choice questions. In many instances, these answers will force a follow-up question that allows the witness to explain.

• There are some cautions to keep in mind. The first is that many forced choice questions are mundane, and can and should be briskly answered with short responses of the yes/no, correct/incorrect variety. A dimensional answer is not a gimmick and will fail if used as such. It is actually the natural way to make a truthful response in a loaded-question framework.

• Many witnesses simply need to be told that it is "okay" to answer a forced-choice question with something other than a one-word reply, if that is the only way to provide a precisely correct answer. Your witness should have this powerful tool available, but not become over-reliant on its use.

• Some questioners will insist that a four-word answer is "non-responsive" since they began by asking for a yes/no only. There are two points for your witness to keep in mind in such an instance. The first is that a question that demands a limited affirmative or negative response can **only** be answered that way. To give an absolute yes or no would not be correct; it would not be true. The question cannot be answered as a simple choice between two poles. Your witness need merely stick to her guns on the point, and she will prevail.

• Questions that go to morality or principle frequently need to be answered with an amplified affirmative or negative response because the tone or implication in the question simply demands it. To the witness, a weak response wouldn't feel sufficiently true. Nor is the downside of facing an objection or rebuke a steep one. A lawyer who asks "You believe in honesty, don't you?" and then objects when the witness replies, "You bet I do!" has already lost the point if the witness clearly meant it when she said it. There is little to fear, as long as the answer is genuine and not a manipulation or an act of faux sincerity.

Inaccurate Words and Phrases Embedded in Questions

• We have said many times that the best witnesses are the best listeners. Listening to questions in a relaxed and focused manner, experienced testifiers learn to attend to the question first, the answer later. One thing they usually do well is manage questions that contain inaccurate or unsuitable terms or phrases.

• In *Hotseat*, the reader is told this with respect to "not quite accurate" characterizing terms:

"You have the right to do this (respond to inaccuracy), of course, since "not quite accurate" is the same as "not true"! If you agree to answer a question that contains inaccurate terms, you are- in a sense- tacitly agreeing that those terms express the truth. You should try to guard against this. On some topics, it may not be "a big deal", but, there may also be instances where (a characterization) is, for listeners, a statement about the kind of person you are. You will not know how these points will be perceived, so bring them up with the questioner when they appear."

• The witness need not answer a question that contains language he finds to be inaccurate. He should do something about it. But what should he do? Well, he has choices:

• Rejecting Improper Terms in Questions: The simplest way for a witness to handle the inclusion of an unacceptable term in a question is to reject it. There are three levels of rejection of questions of this type- and your witness will recognize them

69

instantly upon your describing them. Why? Because they are natural and conversational responses that are used by most of us several times a day in our normal interactions at home and at work.

Here's an example of a question with an inaccurate term included:

Q. "The reason the car wouldn't stop was because the brakes were defective, isn't that right?"

Detect and Reject: First, the witness detects the term which is unsuitable; which he regards as incorrect, thus untrue. Then he rejects the question without explanation.

A. "No, Sir. That isn't right." (Simple Detect and Reject)

Detect and Point: In the second version of the response, he detects the unsuitable term and rejects by pointing out the problem to the questioner.

A. "I wouldn't call those brakes defective." (Detect and Point)

Detect and Correct: In the third version of the response, he detects the unsuitable term and decides to answer the question, but corrects the proposition to make it more accurate.

A. "No, Sir. I think the car failed to stop because the brakes were worn out." (Detect and Correct)

Notice how each of these response types creates a somewhat different kind of tension in the interaction between witness and questioner. Further, each style of answer forces a different kind of follow-up question.

• Give your witness a chance to become more conscious of how he handles questions with inaccurate terms inserted in them. Ask him several such questions containing flag words unique to your case (most cases have several!), and suggest that he answer each question in all three ways.

• The exciting stuff in this work comes when you and the witness explore together what his correcting responses might be with regard to the use of certain volatile terms unique to your case. Usually these are terms that have already turned up in the pleadings or in discovery, and you both know he will be hearing them. Witnesses sometimes feel tremendously empowered when they know how to navigate through this difficult territory.

• If your witness rejects the use of a term, he must be prepared to stand up for himself. He should only reject a term because he thinks it fails as the best expression of the truth. It cannot be a way for him to "game" the questioner. If he does that, he can only lose. However, if he rejects a term because he thinks it is not correct and sticks to his guns on the matter, his word selection must rule. After all, he is the witness; it is his testimony.

In *Hotseat*, the reader is told:

"You may wonder how to do this (reject a term) politely and appropriately, as you will not want to create the wrong impression. You should never quibble or debate or play word games with a questioner. That is not a good idea at all, as most listeners will not like it. But, you still must deal with the use of an inaccurate or incorrect term."

• Urge your witness to the highest level of courtesy when managing this type of situation. Remember, the witness should always be the nicest person in the room.

Hypothetical Questions

• Hypothetical questions create a great deal of anxiety for witnesses (and, often, their lawyers!) because they can work tricks in the mind of the listener. Let's look at an example:

Q. "Mr. Smith, if you had the chance to do it over again, you would have tied that box more tightly onto that trailer, wouldn't you?"

A. "Yes, I would."

It sounds as though Smith might be second-guessing the quality of his box-tying! Is this an admission of negligence?

But, what if Smith had answered more accurately, like this:

A. "If I had known what I know now, that the truck would go over an embankment and the box would be torn loose and hurt Mrs. Jones; I would have glued, welded, and nailed that box to the trailer!"

• In the above answer, Smith correctly re-frames the hypothetical as being considered in the light of hindsight. That would be the truth with almost any hypothetical scenarios your witness will be asked to consider. What-if questions in litigation are almost always being considered in the light of a unique event. They are distorted by the lens of hindsight and often colored with the dark tones of tragedy. The witness should say something about this reality as an accompaniment to any answer he might offer.

In other words, he should limit his answer with a reference to the role of hindsight. Any response not conditioned in this manner would simply not be true.

• Another important thing to teach your witness is that any hypothetical question is bounded by the assumptions the questioner poses at the time the question is asked. The witness might well have used different assumptions, or additional ones, if he had thought of the question, or when he thinks of it later. The assumptions might not make sense when considered later, even though they sound reasonable when the question is asked. Given these confounding truths, the witness can only guess at an answer to the question. When he does answer a hypothetical, he should attach an appropriate proviso, a "guess tag" (as in, "I'm guessing, here, but…") that sounds something like this:

"As I think about your question right here, right now- my best guess is that the answer is X"

or

"Working only with the assumptions you have just given me, I think perhaps X"

• In *Hotseat*, the reader gets this additional tidbit on the subject:

"Some professionals (physicians, scientists, and engineers, for example) testify frequently in cases where their knowledge can be helpful. They are usually called "expert witnesses", and are trained to analyze hypothetical scenarios for the purposes of making legal testimony. They may frequently be obliged to answer this type question. They know how to filter assumptions and how to form and scientifically limit the conclusions that emerge from what-if thinking. They almost always attach appropriate limiting language to their opinions. Proceeding extremely carefully and being tentative in

answering hypothetical questions is not some form of evasion or avoidance, it is intellectual honesty."

• Ask your witness some what-if questions and request that he couch his responses in appropriate limiting language, using "guess tags". This is a skill easily acquired, and he will be much more comfortable if he knows how to do it. He'll be more relaxed and confident, and will proceed with greater resourcefulness on other substantive issues.

The "Guess Tag" Exercise

You need not use the specific issues in your case to give your witness some practice in dealing with hypothetical questions. You can easily use the facts of his life to generate what-if questions. To foster flexibility, invite him to use more than one guess tag to limit his answers. It could sound like this:

Q. "You went to a public high school and then on to the state university, didn't you?"

A. "Yes, sir, I did."

Q. "If you had gone to a private college prep school, you would probably could have gotten yourself a scholarship, right?"

(This is a "probably could have" question. "Woulda, Coulda, Shoulda" questions are just as much hypothetical as any that are more formally proposed! Many witnesses never see them coming...)

A. "I can't answer that. I would only be guessing." (Guess tag and refusal to guess)

As innocuous as the question above sounds, it should be answered with the same discipline as any other. The point is for the witness to learn to recognize these questions. If he wants to answer in a more relaxed way, while still hewing to the rule of knowledge, he might answer something like this:

Q. "If you had gone to a private prep school, you would probably could have gotten yourself a scholarship, right?"

A. "I can only guess about that, but since I had pretty good grades, having a diploma from a good prep school might have made it even better." (Guess tag and a tentative guess)

Notice how the guess, if submitted, should be tentative ("might have made it even better"). This will send the correct message: The truth is that the witness doesn't know what, if anything, would have been different. It's impossible.

Background Facts Missing in Question

• Sometimes a simple-sounding question and its simple-sounding answer will lead a listener to a false conclusion. The reason? The question is being asked without key background facts having been established. Witnesses often recognize these situations and don't know what to do. They may have been told to "answer only the question at hand" and are trying to follow the rules. The too-common result is that something has just been communicated that simply isn't true, and it may or may not be corrected later.

• Some attorneys are themselves taught to instruct witnesses to minimize elaborated or extended answers. If an instance like the one above occurs in a deposition, some lawyers believe that it does no damage to let stand a half-truth asserted in a bad question. They take the position that they can clear it up later in the deposition or deal with it at trial.

• Consider an alternative view: Let the witness handle it right there and right then.

• Witnesses are frequently distracted by situations of this type, and that distraction saps their energy. They also may look for opportunities to repair the damage in a subsequent answer, only to create an awkward addendum to a not-quite-related exchange with the questioner. A witness who knows how to add a "gap tag" (as in "background-information gap") to an answer can usually force a follow-up question. The follow-up permits the necessary information to be delivered. The delivery of additional information in this way is not perceived as gratuitous on the part of the witness. That is because it is requested by the questioner. It is seen by a listener as necessary supplemental information.

• Let's look at some ways for witnesses to add "gap tags":

Q. "Mr. Gomez, isn't it true that your company stopped including the warning booklet with the Model C-3 tool?"

A. "That's true, and we had what we thought was a good reason." (Give the answer. Point out that there is background.)

Note that this response gives the answer first, then adds the gap tag "… and we had what we thought was a good reason." The questioner will feel some pressure to follow up. It is important for the witness to understand that he should confidently give the affirmative or negative first, then, add the tag. To do it the opposite way risks sounding as though he is avoiding the answer.

• Let's look at another type of tag, one that ups the ante:

Q. "Mr. Gomez, isn't it true that your company stopped including the warning booklet with the Model C-3 tool?"

A. "That's true, and there's some background the jury should know about why we did that." (Give the answer. Press for a follow-up.)

As you can see, this gap tag "… there's some background the jury should know…" creates more pressure on the questioner. One caution to your witness about using this device: When the follow-up comes, and it almost has to come, the background information given should be substantive and, in-fact, necessary to understand the preceding answer. This is a very powerful communications device and should not be wasted on excuse-making or insubstantial elaboration. It should be brought into play in service of making complete and accurate testimony only. Skillful testifiers don't waste ammunition.

• Let's look at one more:

> Q. "Mr. Gomez, isn't it true that your company stopped including the warning booklet with the Model C-3 tool?"

> A. "That is true, and there's some interesting research we did on warnings that led to the decision to stop sending them." (Give the answer. Attach the title for the follow-up question.)

Notice how the above answer uses a gap tag "…and there's some interesting research we did on warnings…" that names the topic (Research on Warnings) that the witness believes should now be covered. It creates a demand in the mind of the listener to have that specific gap filled, and − correctly - pressures the questioner to address it.

• This is not a mere game of chicken between witness and attorney. To fail to address missing information is to do a disservice to the truth, so the witness should be allowed to address it. Through the use of gap tags, the witness can both increase the likelihood of being asked to address needed background right away AND neutralize the short version of the answer as a weapon to be used against him later. The second benefit is gained even if the questioner refuses to follow-up.

The "Gap Tag" Exercise

Ask your witness some questions where the lack of background information can make an answer sound like one thing when the truth is quite different. There are numerous examples in everyday life. Most of us are do some version of gap tagging several times a day. Let's take the topic of raising children. If your witness is a parent, you can ask questions like the ones below so that he can practice:

Q. "Have you ever yelled at your child?" (Ignored your child? Been impatient? Been unfair?)

A. "Yes, Sir, I have."

Q. "So, you admit that you have yelled at your child?"

A. "Yes, I sure did. You wouldn't believe what that kid did!"

The above is a simple style of tag that signals that there is important additional information.

How about another example, starting with the second question:

Q. "Mr. Smith, you admit that have treated your child unfairly at times, haven't you?"

A. "I agree that I have, and I'm sure you"ll want to know more about it."

The above is an example of a tag that presses for a follow-up. It creates tension.

Another example:

Q. "Mr. Smith, you admit that your neighbors have criticized your child rearing practices, haven't they?"

A. "A couple of them did, that's right. We had a talk in my driveway about "Tough Love" that same day."

This answer is a tag that gives a name for the material that will fill the gap. Once again, there is pressure on the questioner to follow up.

You should try to get your witness to see the power in tags like these examples, tags that "tee up" the follow-up question. They allow the witness to fill in the material pursuant to a request, rather than doing so in a way that could sound like a rush-to-explain. Follow-up questions are, of necessity, often open-ended. That gives the witness room to narrate, to tell a story.

Inaccurate or Incomplete Context in Question

• Recall a point made earlier in this book: If a listener hears testimony with insufficient contextual information, the listener will fill in the blanks, and he might fill them in incorrectly. For that reason and more, this book is biased towards preparing witnesses to make complete answers to questions and to testifying to their truth in full rather than in part. Happily, thorough preparation on the facts and then plenty of skill-building work is exactly what arms witnesses best to do just that.

• When your witness is armed with clearly expressed and meaningfully characterized factual testimony that he is ready to deliver with appropriate background and context information, then he needs to be able to get it into the record! Unfortunately, opposing counsel is not likely to ask for it. Opposing counsel is more likely to ask leading questions that have a bias towards his view of things. Some of those questions may be barren as to context or, instead, have inaccurate contextual references. Your witness needs to know how to use the instant of such questions as the leverage for putting things right.

Here's a few tips, a couple of which you have seen before:

• Detect and Reject

Example: Q. "Mr. Jones, the training for your job as safety manager seems to only have involved a single one-week course; is that correct?"

Example Answer: (Reject only)

"I don't think that's correct."

Some questions lend themselves more readily to such responses. In this instance the rejecting statement is so firm that the questioner may have to worry just a bit in deciding what to do next. Perhaps he will follow up with a demand for an explanation, perhaps launch another closed-end question? Something. But, he must do something. He can't let that answer stand.

Your witness has answered firmly on a subject that is important. He (and you) knew a question like this was coming. He is ready with the truth. But, he isn't rushing an important point of truth out in a gratuitous way, at the risk of seeming defensive. Instead, correctly, he is letting the questioner do the work. He will almost surely get to make his answer in a moment, and he'll be free to put it in context, to speak the whole truth.

• Detect and Correct

Example: Q. "Mr. Jones, the training for your job as safety manager seems to only have involved a single one-week course; is that correct?"

Example Answer: (Apologize; Reject and Correct with an accurately stated fact)

"I'm sorry, I don't think that describes my training at all; but I certainly did take a safety related classroom course."

Notice that the above example includes an apology before the rejection/correction response. The apology is important. It sets a standard of courtesy for the exchange that is highly courteous, even deferential. But, there is something else. In ordinary conversation at work or with a friend, an apology at the beginning of a statement earns a speaker a certain amount of immunity if that speaker needs to say something a listener might find unpleasant. ("I'm sorry to have to say this, but I just ran over your dog.") In a deposition or at a trial, some of the same dynamics come into play. This is a socially appropriate way to contradict the questioner. It is inoffensive. Teach your witness the power of the apology.

- Detect and De-Construct

    Example: Q. "Mr. Jones, the training for your job as safety manager seems to only have involved a single one-week course; is that correct?"

    Example Answer: (Reject and Deconstruct the question, addressing some essential element of it)

    "No, my safety management training took a lot more than that."

Deconstructing a question to one essential element created a chance for this witness to make a strong affirmative statement. Interestingly, the response also is sufficiently imprecise ("...took a lot more...") that it cries out for further inquiry. It is almost as if the questioner has an implied duty to follow-up. That, of course, is what our witness is hoping for: a chance to put the story of his training into context. As your witness becomes more comfortable with his testimony, he may develop the ability shown by the fellow answering the question in this example. Mr. Jones knows how to leave something hanging in an answer, something enticing.

- Reject and Reconstruct

    Example: Q. "Mr. Jones, the training for your job as safety manager seems to only have involved a single one-week course; is that correct?"

    Example Answer: (Reject and Reconstruct with a contrary proposition, including needed background and context)

"Actually, the training for my job as safety manager included ten years working as a safety inspector and supervisor in several different areas, as well as that one week course on applying OSHA Regulations."

Here, Mr. Jones takes a risk, but sometimes the proposition in a question ("You basically have no training for your job.") is so preposterous that a witness may be moved to mount a completely contrary one, and then complete the thought with the information necessary to understand why the question was so ridiculous. Perhaps you think he should have opened with an apology, too. It might have blunted the bright edge of this response, but would have been less confrontive.

Give your witness the opportunity to hear and then answer some questions by applying one of the "Reject and..." tools to his responses. This will make him feel more comfortable that he knows how to address lack of context in questions.

- Importantly, most of the rejection devices we have discussed here will create opportunities for witnesses to explain things without seeming defensive, without making speeches that may draw objection. Most of the time, a well-crafted rejecting answer will trigger a follow-up of some sort. That is when the explanation can be delivered.

• The goal is always the same, no matter the communications technique being applied. It is that of making testimony that is the truth, the whole truth, and nothing but the truth.

The "Missing Context" Exercise

Create some questions for your witness so that she can practice using the "Detect and Reject" tools. You should try to invent some examples that you can ask repeatedly, giving her the chance to answer the same question using all four versions of a truthful response. It will help her grasp the essence of the concept as well as giving her a feel for the different effects created by the different response forms. You may wish to come up with material that emerges from your case, but it isn't necessary to do so. Once again, real life gives us everything we need.

Have you ever been in public and discovered your clothing was unzipped or un-buttoned? Let's imagine that your witness gives you a little story about just that: She was doing a presentation for a client and didn't realize that a button had come off her blouse leaving it open more than a bit too much. Some embarrassment followed.

Now, you simply turn that into an out of context question:

Q. "So, you once had a client report to your boss that she was upset by your revealing blouse, isn't that true?"

A. "No, Sir. That isn't true at all." (Detect and Reject)

Now let's try an example with a correction:

A. "No, Sir. I once had a client tell my boss a story about a problem I had with a blouse button." (Reject and Correct)

Let's do one with a de-construction:

A. "No, Sir. But, I did once have a funny problem with a blouse button at a meeting." (Reject and de-construct)

Finally, let's allow our witness to re-construct the proposition completely:

A. "No, Sir. Actually, after I won a new account, the client told my boss that he was impressed with how humorously I handled a major wardrobe malfunction that came up right in the middle of the presentation." (Reject and re-construct)

Please allow your witness to actually practice using these tools. Repetition is the key to success.

Conclusion

We hope that you have found some useful ideas in this short book. No doubt you realize that some witnesses will take much more readily than others to systematic preparation of this type. The more general communications handbook, *Hotseat*, can serve as a companion to your in-person education of your witness. We hope you read it, and consider giving all your witnesses a copy.

One other thing is hoped: That you will learn these skills, have this manual ready at hand, and be able to help your witness during preparation for testimony if he becomes anxious or stuck. Let yourself truly be wise counsel in the sense of being a source of wisdom and support. Let yourself become deeply invested in your witness' success. You will both profit.